Striking Financial Balance in Marriage

I0558390

Expert Strategies for Achieving Financial Harmony and Security as Couples

Adegboya S. Aduragbemi

INTRODUCTION

Money is more than just money; it's a language that we speak in every aspect of our lives, and nowhere is it likely that its influence is felt more deeply than in a marriage. However, handling the complexities of money in a married relationship frequently prompts concerns about goal-setting, investing, saving, and budgeting. "Finance FAQ in Marriage" is a helpful resource for married couples who are looking for direction, comprehension, and real-world advice when negotiating the financial challenges they face together.

This book contains a wealth of information on frequently asked topics, thoughtful responses, and professional guidance specific to the intricacies of marriage-related finances. Couples may handle the complexity of finances with grace and purpose by using our actionable assistance, empathy, and understanding to address any subject, from the menial responsibilities of budgeting to the momentous considerations of retirement planning.

"Finance FAQ in Marriage" provides couples with a road map for creating financial harmony, accomplishing common goals, and fortifying their marriage with relevant tales, real-life events, and evidence-based tactics. Whether you are a newlywed attempting to balance your money or a seasoned couple looking to align your financial destiny, this book offers priceless ideas and valuable tools to help you face the challenges of finance head-on and with courage.

May you find comfort in other people's experiences that you have shared, inspiration in the knowledge of professionals, and the guts to accept financial harmony as a means of achieving more fulfillment and connection in your marriage as you go out on this path of research and discovery.

Together, let's travel through the ageless dilemmas, complex issues, and exquisite aspects of money in marriage.

Chapter One

Set your priority right before going into the relationship

Sample of relationship that was destroyed due to financial failure

Sarah and Michael were a prominent couple in the fast-paced city of New York. After meeting in college, they fell madly in love and decided to take on the world as a team. Michael was a prosperous investment banker, and Sarah was a focused marketing professional. Their future appeared promising, limitless, and full of possibilities.

Their lifestyles grew along with their jobs. They traveled the world in elegance, ate at Michelin-starred restaurants, and resided in an opulent apartment overlooking Central Park. But beneath the surface of prosperity, there was a sinister truth: their finances were getting out of hand.

Sarah had no idea that Michael had been taking chances with his investments in the hopes of winning significant and securing their financial future. However, misfortune did not favor them, as their investments started to falter, ultimately putting them deeply in debt.

Sarah first noticed small changes: late payments, credit cards that were fully utilized, and contentious exchanges over money. She made an effort to talk sense into Michael's head, asking him to be more accountable and open about their money, but he dismissed her worries and assured her that everything would work out.

Their relationship deteriorated along with their financial problems. The once-in-love pair grew aloof and spiteful toward one another. Michael's risky actions made Sarah feel deceived, and her constant pestering about money made him feel smothered.

Once a representation of their prosperity, their penthouse was turned into a jail by their design. They were compelled to sell their possessions and downsize to a modest apartment in the suburbs because they could no longer afford their extravagant lifestyle.

Sarah and Michael had reached their breaking point due to their overwhelming debt and dashed hopes. Their once-loved and trusting marriage fell apart due to their mounting debt. Claimant to have brought the other down; they filed for divorce.

Years later, Sarah and Michael coincidentally crossed paths once more. They made polite small talk, but the fondness and warmth they had once shared had vanished. They couldn't help but ponder what would have happened if they had put their love above their money as they turned to leave each other.

This story serves as an example of how financial challenges can put a strain on even the most solid marriages, emphasizing the value of open communication, honesty, and support from one another when handling economic difficulties in a marriage.

Sample of relationship that was built due to a well-organized

finance

Two driven individuals in the vibrant metropolis of London discovered that their paths to success were diverging. Emily was a gifted financial analyst who had always aspired to be successful in the investing industry. An experienced businessman, James was committed to starting his empire from scratch. They had no idea that their paths would eventually cross in the most peculiar ways.

Emily was a rising star in a respected investing firm, well-known for her astute observation of profitable enterprises and sharp mind. Conversely, James was a brilliant businessman who had a talent for transforming creative concepts into successful ventures. They met at a well-known networking event, and right away, they felt a strong desire to succeed and a common goal. After exchanging business cards and striking up a lively discussion, Emily and James realized they had similar interests in entrepreneurship and money. Their shared intelligence, aspirations, and outlook on the future drew them together. They started working together, exchanging ideas, and looking into ways to combine their skills and knowledge over the ensuing weeks.

Driven by a common desire for success and financial independence, their relationship took off in the world of stock markets and boardrooms. Alongside each other, they overcame obstacles and shared triumphs as they successfully navigated the complexities of the commercial world.

The entrepreneurial zeal of James's and Emily's analytical abilities was the reason why they made a powerful combination that helped them succeed both in their business and career life. Their relationship deepened as they pursued the same objectives because of their admiration for one another, respect for one another, and similar future visions.

Amid their career achievements, Emily and James came to understand that their bond went beyond a corporate collaboration and instead represented a more profound and intense love. In front of friends, family, and coworkers, they exchanged vows in an opulent ceremony, securing their dedication to one another and their common goals.

Years later, Emily and James were at the top of their game, their names instantly recognizable in the financial and business worlds as symbols of creativity, honesty, and quality. Their romantic tale stood as a tribute to the strength of ambition, teamwork, and respect for one another in creating a prosperous partnership, one that was genuinely founded on money but was maintained by love, trust, and steadfast support for one another.

This narrative demonstrates how a couple's mutual love of business and finance can foster not only their professional success but also a more robust bond over time between them on a personal level.

Chapter Two

Striking balance in marriage

As a couple, how do we go about budgeting and financial planning?

Set common objectives, talk about priorities, and work together as a team to create a budget that takes into account the needs and values of both partners when approaching financial planning and budgeting. To guarantee financial transparency and alignment, come to choices collectively regarding savings, investments, and spending.

If our financial habits or opinions around money differ, what should we do?

Have frank discussions to learn about one other's viewpoints if your financial practices or attitudes regarding money differ. Establish common ground, make concessions where needed, and draft a budget that honors the objectives and values of each partner.

How can we resolve issues or disagreements over money in our marriage?

Use active listening, empathy, and compromise to resolve financial conflicts. Instead of blaming others or getting defensive, concentrate on coming up with solutions that address the needs and worries of both parties. If you need assistance with complicated financial matters, get outside assistance from a financial expert or counselor.

Should a married couple share their funds or maintain them apart?

Every couple has different circumstances and tastes; thus, it is up to them to decide whether to combine or keep their finances separate. While some couples want to keep their accounts separate to preserve their individuality and liberty, others want to integrate them for ease and openness. Make a choice based on an honest discussion of your alternatives that will benefit your relationship.

Chapter Three

Questions about some other crucial factors that affect

communication in marriage

In our marriage, how do we handle different earnings or financial contributions?

Discuss expectations, obligations, and contributions openly and sincerely in order to address unequal incomes or financial contributions. If sharing expenses equally or proportionately based on income seems fair and reasonable to both spouses, then think about doing so.

What are some joint savings and investing tactics?

As a pair, save and invest by establishing mutual financial objectives, automating savings contributions, and spreading out your holdings to reduce risk. Together, decide what your short and long-term financial priorities are. You should also periodically examine and make any necessary adjustments to your savings and investing strategy.

How do we handle money problems or debt in our marriage?

Deal with debt or money problems by working as a team to overcome them. Make a plan for paying off debt, give high-interest loans and credit cards top priority, and, if necessary, look into debt consolidation or refinancing possibilities. To create a plan for handling debt and strengthening your relationship's financial stability, get assistance from a financial counselor or advisor.

What should we do if our priorities or financial goals diverge?

Have polite, honest talks to grasp one other's viewpoints better if your financial objectives or priorities disagree. Seek out places where the demands and goals of the two partners can be balanced by making concessions or finding common ground. To accommodate varying priorities in your marriage, think about establishing both shared and individual financial goals.

As a couple, how do we deal with unforeseen costs or financial emergencies?

Establish an emergency fund and talk about backup plans in advance to deal with unforeseen costs or financial emergencies. Together, decide how to distribute money in an emergency and give priority to creating a financial safety net to guard against unforeseen circumstances.

In our marriage, how can we support one another's financial objectives and goals?

Encourage, hold each other accountable, and lend a helpful hand when necessary to support one another's financial ambitions. Together, we celebrate significant events and accomplishments and collaborate to get beyond roadblocks and hurdles in the way of achieving financial success.

As a couple, how do we handle daily spending and home budgeting?

Establish a joint budget that details all sources of income, fixed and variable costs, and savings targets in order to manage daily spending and household budgeting effectively. Regularly review your budget, monitor your spending, and make any modifications to ensure that your finances are stable and in line with your objectives.

What are some ways to talk to our partner about money without getting into a fight?

It's essential to have open communication, active listening skills, and a nonjudgmental attitude while talking about money with your partner to avoid arguments. Select a moment when both parties are composed and concentrated, voice issues using "I" statements, and approach the discussion with compassion and understanding.

How can we attain financial honesty in our marriage, and what part does it play?

In order to foster alignment and trust in a marriage, financial transparency is crucial. By being honest with your partner about your income, expenses, obligations, and economic goals, you can achieve financial transparency. Make choices as a group

17

and distribute access to financial papers, investment accounts, and bank accounts.

What actions can we take to guarantee stability and financial security for our future together as a couple?

Make sure that your future together is stable and secure financially by giving priority to investments, savings, and insurance that guards against unforeseen circumstances. Make a thorough financial strategy that takes into account both your short and long-term objectives. Then, as your situation changes over time, evaluate and update your plan on a regular basis.

When it comes to discretionary spending, such as hobbies or leisure, how do we address variances in financial priorities or values?

Compromise and understanding are necessary for managing disparities in financial priorities. Together, you should explore your values and preferences around discretionary spending and work out a compromise that will let both of you pursue your interests and hobbies without jeopardizing your financial security. Think about allocating a specific sum of money each month for luxuries and decide how it will be used.

Chapter Four

Securing your marriage from external influence

As a couple, how do we handle big purchases or investments when it comes to money?

Talk about priorities, goals, and possible risks and advantages while making financial decisions as a partnership. Investigate your choices, consult one another, and jointly decide on a course of action that will satisfy both parties and be consistent with your long-term financial strategy.

As a couple, how can we set attainable and realistic financial goals?

As a pair, prioritize specified, measurable, attainable, relevant, and timebound (SMART) goals to set realistic and achievable financial goals. To keep yourself motivated and focused on your economic trip, break down larger objectives into smaller milestones, track progress on a regular basis, and share successes with your group.

How do we handle anxiety or tension related to money in our marriage?

Establish a welcoming climate that encourages candid dialogue and mutual assistance in order to alleviate feelings of financial stress or anxiety. Together, explore coping mechanisms, validate one another's emotions, and, if necessary, seek professional assistance from a financial adviser or counselor to create a strategy for stress management and resilience building.

As a marriage, how do we deal with windfalls or unforeseen financial gains?

Prior to deciding how to use windfalls or unforeseen financial benefits, have a collaborative discussion about objectives and goals. Think about putting money toward investments, savings, paying off debt, or having joint experiences that support your long-term financial goals and values as a partnership.

If one partner is more responsible or financially wise than the other, what should we do?

Take advantage of the chance for mutual learning and development if one partner is more financially astute or prudent than the other. Discuss financial literacy openly and sincerely, exchange information and resources, and cooperate to create a standard grasp of economic concepts and procedures.

How do we resolve discrepancies in our marital spending habits or values on money?

Reaching a consensus, being truthful with one another, and compromising is necessary for managing disparities in financial values or spending patterns. Talk about each other's priorities, decide on joint spending objectives, and set limits or rules for expenditures that honor the needs and values of both partners.

In a marriage, how may one handle both individual and joint accounts?

In a married relationship, managing individual and joint accounts calls for open communication, mutual trust, and agreement on how money will be handled. Establish rules for the distribution and access of funds to guarantee openness and accountability. Agree on which costs will be paid for jointly and which will be handled separately.

How can we guard against financial infidelity or dishonesty in our marriage?

Make open communication, responsibility, and transparency about money a priority to safeguard your marriage against financial infidelity or dishonesty. To avoid miscommunications or betrayals of trust, be forthright about your financial status, provide others access to financial records and accounts, and engage in conversations about significant financial choices.

How can creating financial objectives improve our marriage?

By promoting alignment, teamwork, and a shared future vision, financial goal-setting is essential to the health of your marriage. Together, identify and work toward SMART (specific, measurable, realistic, relevant, and timebound) financial goals. Celebrate your progress and accomplishments to reaffirm your commitment to a profitable collaboration.

How do we handle worries regarding unequal income distribution or financial contributions in our marriage?

Have polite, candid discussions regarding each partner's role, contributions, and financial duties in the relationship to ease worries about unequal financial contributions or income discrepancies. To address income differences over time, take into account techniques for an equitable allocation of expenses, such as a proportionate contribution depending on income or other considerations, and look into prospects for professional growth and advancement.

When one partner is a spender, and the other is a saver, how can we manage money decisions?

Striking a balance and making concessions are necessary when managing the disparities in wealth between spenders and savers. Talk candidly about your values, priorities, and financial aspirations. Think about creating a budget that permits each partner to save money and spend it on items that make them happy or fulfilled. To maintain economic stability while preserving the freedom to pursue personal preferences, establish boundaries, and decide on spending caps for discretionary items.

If one partner has been concealing purchases or debts, how do we deal with financial infidelity?

Honesty, accountability, and trust-building are necessary while dealing with financial infidelity. Discuss any concealed debts or purchases in an honest and nonjudgmental manner and collaborate to determine the underlying causes of the behavior. Make a plan to deal with the financial fallout and stop this kind of thing from happening again. To help you through the process and regain trust, think about consulting with a financial expert or counselor.

How can we handle conflict and financial strain without having a harmful effect on our relationship?

Effective communication and problem-solving abilities are necessary for handling financial stress and conflicts. Engage in empathy-building, active listening, and respect for one another's viewpoints. Instead of blaming others or getting defensive, concentrate on coming up with solutions together. When feelings are running high, take a break and bring up the topic again when everyone is calmer and more open to working out a compromise.

How should prenuptial agreements be incorporated into our joint financial planning?

Prenuptial agreements are a valuable instrument for outlining expectations around money and safeguarding assets in the case of a divorce. Discuss with your partner transparently and openly about the potential of a prenuptial agreement. It would be best if you also thought about getting legal advice to understand your options and the legal ramifications fully.

Respect each other's priorities and concerns by being sensitive and discreet during the talk.

How can we fortify our bond and establish a feeling of purpose together by using financial goals?

By bringing your goals together and cooperating to create a shared future vision, financial goals might help you and your partner grow closer. Establish goals like debt repayment, emergency fund building, or dream trip savings that align with your values and priorities as a partnership. To reaffirm your commitment to one another and your collaboration, acknowledge and celebrate your progress together.

What actions can we take to make sure that our financial choices align with our relationship objectives and long-term values?

Regularly review your priorities and reevaluate your financial plan to make sure your money actions are in line with your long-term values and relationship goals. Openly discuss your hopes and worries with one another, and work together to reach decisions that are in line with your shared future vision. If necessary, get advice from a financial professional or counselor to create a plan that upholds your morals and improves your relationship.

In our financial planning, how can we find a balance between living for the moment and saving for the future?

Finding mutually agreeable compromises and prioritizing your short and long-term goals is vital to striking a balance between living life to the fullest and conserving for the future. Set away money for future needs and objectives, but also devote a portion of your salary to activities and luxuries that make you happy and fulfilled in the moment. Make sure you are moving toward your short and long-term goals by reviewing and adjusting your financial plan on a regular basis.

How can a couple manage their debt, particularly if one of them has a large amount of debt from a previous relationship?

Transparency, communication, and a cooperative attitude to debt repayment are necessary for managing debt as a marriage. Talk openly about each other's debts, including the total amount owing, the interest rate, and the payback schedule. Make a plan for jointly paying off debt, giving priority to high-interest debt, and, if appropriate, looking into consolidation or refinancing options. Establish reasonable deadlines and goals for paying off debt, and encourage one another along the way.

If one partner has a more significant income or wealth than the other, how should we go about financial planning?

Treat financial planning delicately and with consideration for the circumstances and contributions of each spouse. Make decisions together that take into account the needs and aspirations of both partners after having candid conversations about financial expectations, obligations, and goals. To create a strategy that optimizes your combined assets and promotes your long-term financial security as a couple, think about speaking with a financial advisor.

After getting an inheritance or other monetary windfall during our marriage, how should we handle it, particularly if one partner has different plans for it?

Treat inheritances and financial windfalls with tact and consideration for one another's objectives and desires. Talk openly about the inheritance or windfall and how it should be invested, spent, and handled. To explore choices and create a plan that fits both partners' goals and values as a couple, think about speaking with a financial expert or counselor.

How important are continuing education and financial education for efficient money management in a couple?

To efficiently manage funds as a pair and lay the groundwork for long-term financial security, financial education, and continuous learning are crucial. Together, commit to learning about personal finance subjects like investing, retirement planning, and budgeting. It would help if you also looked for books, seminars, or other resources that can help you become more financially literate and capable of making better decisions.

Make wise choices and work together to overcome financial obstacles by utilizing your knowledge and experience.

How can we improve our relationship and enhance our bond as a couple by using milestone celebrations and financial goal-setting?

Make the most of milestone celebrations and financial goalsetting as chances to improve your relationship and enhance your bond. Together, identify and strive toward common values and aspirations while setting joint financial goals. Commemorate your victories along the road by praising your development, treating yourself to worthwhile events, and thanking each other for your mutual contributions to your financial prosperity.

In light of our shifting circumstances and stages of life, how can we make sure that our financial decisions are

consistent with our shared beliefs and priorities as a couple?

By periodically reviewing your objectives and reevaluating your financial plan, you can make sure that your financial decisions are in line with your values and priorities. Discuss your hopes, worries, and evolving situation honestly and openly with others. Then, jointly decide on actions that will best serve your shared future vision. Seek advice from dependable mentors or advisors, and exercise flexibility and adaptability as you both negotiate life's unexpected turns.

Chapter Five

How does technology affect communication in a marriage, and how

can we make sure it strengthens rather than weakens our bond?

How do we manage gifts of money or inheritances that we have received while getting married?

Discuss expectations, objectives, and possible uses for the money with your spouse while handling inheritances or financial gifts received throughout your marriage. Together, come to decisions that are in line with your long-term financial goals and your beliefs as a marriage.

How do we deal with monetary difficulties brought on by outside causes like job loss or economic downturns?

To effectively navigate financial issues arising from external circumstances, a couple must possess adaptability, resilience, and mutual support. Make a plan for handling unforeseen circumstances, including losing your job or experiencing a downturn in the economy, and give priority to accumulating an emergency fund to pay for necessities during hard times. As a team, weather the storm by relying on one another for emotional support and looking into opportunities for financial aid or counseling when necessary.

In the framework of our marriage, what lessons about morals and financial responsibility can we impart to our kids?

By modeling sound financial practices and having candid discussions about money as a family, you can teach your kids about financial responsibility and morals. Engage your kids in age-appropriate conversations about saving, spending, and budgeting. Please give them the tools they need to make wise financial decisions by giving them the opportunity for experiential learning and real-world application.

As we get older in our marriage together, how do we handle worries about financial security and retirement planning?

Have frank discussions about your retirement expectations, fears, and ambitions in order to ease worries about financial security and retirement preparation. Assess your existing monetary status, look into retirement savings and investment choices, and create a plan that fits your lifestyle and your shared retirement goals.

In our marriage, how can we strike a balance between our immediate financial needs and our long-term financial goals?

Prioritizing needs above wants, establishing precise deadlines and goals, and making calculated choices that support your long-term financial goals are all necessary to strike a balance between short-term and long-term financial planning. Maintain a regular review and revision process for your financial plan to account for evolving situations and guarantee that your immediate and long-term needs are being satisfied.

How can we utilize financial planning as a tool to improve our future together and fortify our marriage?

By encouraging cooperation, trust, and a shared future vision, financial planning can be a valuable tool in strengthening your marriage. Achieving financial success and stability requires setting shared objectives, coming to financial decisions as a team, and cooperating. You may lay a solid basis for a happy and fulfilling life together by placing a high value on open communication, transparency, and mutual support.

What are some methods for managing shared costs, including rent, electricity, and groceries?

Managing shared spending necessitates clearly defining each partner's role and expectations. Make a budget that details all of the shared costs and contributions, and decide who will be in charge of handling the household money and how bills will be paid. To ensure that invoices are paid on time, think about creating joint accounts for shared costs and automating payments.

How should we go about making financial plans for significant life events like having kids, purchasing a home, or saving for retirement?

To prepare financially for significant life events, first determine your objectives, then project the associated costs and devise a savings strategy to meet them. Look into your options and potential financing methods for significant expenses, such as retirement account contributions, a college fund set up for kids, or a down payment on a home. A financial mentor can help you generate a detailed strategy that is suited to your unique situation and needs.

As a couple, how do we deal with monetary setbacks like job loss or unforeseen expenses?

Resilience, adaptability, and cooperation are necessary for overcoming financial setbacks. To weather the storm, go over your budget and rank the most significant costs. Look at ways to temporarily lower expenses or bring in more money, such as taking on a part-time job or reducing discretionary spending.

Rely on one another for emotional support while concentrating on working together to discover answers to the problems.

In situations where one partner is financially dependent on the other, like when one is unemployed or disabled, what steps should we take?

Treat the situation with kindness, support, and open communication if one couple depends on the other for money. Have a conversation about each other's expectations, worries, and requirements for financial support. Then, work together to develop a strategy that will meet the needs of both partners while preserving the family's financial security. To overcome the obstacles jointly, look into opportunities for extra money or support, such as disability insurance or unemployment benefits, and, if necessary, seek outside assistance.

In the framework of our marriage, how can we impart financial freedom and responsibility to our kids?

Model financial independence and responsibility for your kids by being a good role model and including them in age-appropriate financial conversations and activities. From an early age, promote budgeting, saving, and ethical spending practices. Also, it offers opportunities for practical economic education and decision-making. Teachable moments can be created from routine tasks like grocery shopping and bill paying to convey important lessons about financial freedom and literacy.

If one partner owns property or has significant financial holdings, how do we safeguard our marriage and assets in the event of a divorce or separation?

It takes careful planning and thoughtful evaluation of your legal choices to safeguard your marriage and possessions in the incident of a divorce or separation. Openly and honestly discuss prenuptial or postnuptial agreements with your partner. It would be best if you also spoke with a lawyer to learn about the legal ramifications and your rights. Make choices that take into account the interests and goals of both partners by approaching the discussion with tact and respect for each other's priorities and concerns.

About the Author

ADEGBOYE S. ADURAGBEMI is a manager, business administrator, entrepreneur, and motivational speaker in Africa. ADEGBOYE has his BA from Yale University, IPMA from Adonai University, and a Masters in Business Administration (MBA) from the University of Salford, Manchester.

He was born in South Africa but is presently based in Nigeria as a c motivational speaker and marriage counselor in institutions, sectors, and seminars with young and upcoming managers all over Africa.

Acknowledgments

I want to express my sincere gratitude to everyone who helped with the "FAQ on Communication in Marriage." Throughout this journey, their encouragement, insight, and support have been priceless.

I want to start by acknowledging the fact that, without God, this guide wouldn't have been possibly achieved.

And also to my spouse, who has always been motivating and supportive in making this task successful, I will always love and appreciate you.

I have many couples to appreciate who have shared their experiences, challenges, and victories with me over the years. Your openness, weakness, and tenacity have enhanced the book's pages and provided priceless insights into the difficulties of marriage communication.

My sincere gratitude goes out to my family and friends for their continuous support and encouragement during this journey. Your wise advice, tolerance, and words of support have helped me get through the complicated process of writing and releasing this book. I sincerely thank the specialists and experts who have so kindly offered their knowledge and skills in marriage and communication. Your advice and thoughts have improved this book's quality and depth, and I really appreciate your contributions.

Finally, I would like to express my profound gratitude to all of the readers of this work. As you journey through the process of communication in your marriage, I hope that the knowledge, direction, and encouragement provided within these pages will be a source of inspiration and empowerment for you. I sincerely appreciate your help.

www.ingramcontent.com/pod-product-compliance
Lightning Source LLC
Chambersburg PA
CBHW051249120626
46547CB00014B/1870